Copyright © 2021 Katherine H. Brown

ISBN: 978-1-7367183-4-6

All rights reserved. No part of this publication may be reproduced, stored or transmitted in any form or by any means, electronic, mechanical, photocopying, recording, scanning, or otherwise without written permission from the publisher. It is illegal to copy this book, post it to a website, or distribute it by any other means without permission.

For daughters
and their dreams.

So, you think you've picked your dress.

You're not alone.

Girls from age ten to forty-five have been dreaming of their perfect wedding for decades.

With this wedding planning journal, you can keep track of those plans. And how fun will it be to look back and see if your plans have changed or remained steadfast?

Now, let's take it a step further than flowers.

How much better will it be for your perfect wedding, to stand at the altar and know that you've prepared your heart for more than that one big day?

Instead, to know that you've prepared your heart for a lifetime of marriage and not just your head for a wedding ceremony.

This planning journal was created for you, dreamers.

All of you!

All ages.

And it has multiple sections so that there is room for changing your mind. A girl's biggest prerogative.

Have fun. Dream big. And go deeper than the decorations.

# My Dream Wedding

## Plan A

Name: _____

Age: _____

Date: _____

*You are altogether beautiful, my darling; there is no flaw in you.*

*Song of Solomon 4:7*

# THE DRESS.

Describe your dream wedding dress. Is it fluffy? Flowy? Short? Long? Smooth? Sequined? What is the dress of your wildest dreams?

_____

_____

_____

_____

Draw or attach a picture of your dream dress below.

"Do not let your adornment
be merely outward—arranging the hair,
wearing gold, or putting on fine apparel—
rather let it be the hidden person of the heart,
with the incorruptible beauty of a gentle and
quiet spirit, which is very precious in the sight of
God."

1 Peter 3:3-4

# THE HAIR.

You have pictured it for ages, admired it on movie stars, been trying out the style in your bedroom. Updo? Curls? Flowing locks? Will it require a full can of hairspray to stay in place? Or are you going for a more relaxed and natural look? What is your wedding hair style?

_____

_____

_____

_____

Draw or attach a picture of your dream wedding hair below.

There is no shame to wanting to look beautiful on your wedding day. But true beauty runs deeper than a pretty dress and flawless hair.

Just as God reminds us not to focus more on our outward appearance than on our inner character, it is also important that we don't fall into the trap of designing a beautiful wedding without any regard to the heart of ourself and our husband-to-be.

Characteristics are defined as qualities that serve to identify a person.

What characteristics do you have that will make you a good wife?

_____

_____

_____

_____

What characteristics do you need God to continue to grow in you?

_____

_____

_____

*"But the fruit of the Spirit is love, joy, peace, longsuffering, gentleness, goodness, faith, Meekness, temperance: against such there is no law."*

*Galatians 5:22-23*

# The Person

What characteristics, or fruits, will you be looking for in first a boyfriend and eventually a husband? Is he kind? Smart? Sober? Reliable? Gentle? Strong? Creative?
List as many as you can that are important to you!

_____

_____

_____

_____

_____

Which of these characteristics are NOT negotiable, or absolute must-haves?

_____

_____

_____

_____

*Iron sharpeneth iron; so a man sharpeneth the countenance of his friend.*

*Proverbs 27:17*

# The Wedding Party

Bridesmaids, groomsmen, flower girls, and ring bearers oh my!

Make a list of who will stand with you on your big day, and then ask yourself, do they support your relationship with your soon-to-be-partner AND with God? Do they speak truth to you? Encourage you?

_____

_____

_____

_____

_____

_____

_____

_____

_____

_____

*"and having shod your feet with the preparation  
of the gospel of peace;"*

*Ephesians 6:15*

# THE SHOES

Heels? Flats? Wedges? Barefoot? Foot jewelry? Let's hear it. What kind of shoes do you imagine walking down the aisle in?

_____

_____

Better yet, draw or attach a picture of them below.




Now consider your feet, on which those shoes will go. Which direction are they taking you? Toward God or away? When you get into any relationship, this should always be a question you ask yourself, are you being led toward God, or away? If away, you need to put on some running shoes instead and get out of there ASAP!

*The grass withers, the flower fades,
But the word of our God stands forever."*

*Isaiah 40:8*

# THE FLOWERS

Silk? Fresh? Roses? Lilies? Red? Pink? Yellow? Blue? There are so many options. List your first choice for flowers below.

Bride's Bouquet: _____

Wedding Party: _____

Flower Girl Basket: _____

Boutonnieres: _____

Decorations: _____

Reception Centerpieces: _____

Draw or attach an image of your bridal bouquet below.

No matter which you choose, beautiful though they may be, they will not last forever.

The fresh will wilt; die.

The silk will fade, or be put away in a dusty attic.

Their fates are as numerous as their petals.

But as Isaiah points out, the word of God is forever.

Have you been in the word?

Have you spent time with God concerning your future?

Is it written on your heart?

What about the heart of your spouse?

Pray that God provides a man of God's own word, someone who can encourage you and study with you, learning God's will for your lives as you grow together in faith. Write that prayer below.

*The flowers appear on the earth; The time of singing has come, And the voice of the turtledove Is heard in our land.*

*Song of Solomon 2:12*

*Let us come before His presence with thanksgiving;
Let us shout joyfully to Him with psalms.*

*Psalm 95:2*

# THE MUSIC

Oh, the music! An opportunity to set the tone. Traditional? Uniqu?. Special songs with special meanings? DJ? Playlist? Pianist?

Your choices may be hard to make, listening to song after song and trying to pick a favorite, or you may know without a second thought what you want played during every part of the ceremony.

Music for guests to be seated? _____

_____

Music for family to be seated? _____

_____

Music for flower girl and ring bearer? _____

_____

Music for wedding party? _____

_____

Music during bride's entrance? _____

_____


Music as bride and groom exit? _____

_____


Music to be played at reception? _____

_____

_____

_____

You may have your own ideas about the best music, but don't forget to check in with your groom when you are finalizing wedding plans.

His ideas may surprise you.

*In His hand* are *the deep places of the earth;*
*The heights of the hills* are *His also.*
*The sea* is *His, for He made it;*
*And His hands formed the dry land.*

*Psalm 95:4-5*

# THE VENUE

Have you pictured the place where you will stand before family and friends and receive a new name? Is it the church you grew up in? A beautiful beach holding special memories? Indoors? Outdoors? Large and spacious? Small and cozy?

Indoors/Outdoors? _____

Location: _____

Large/Small: _____

No matter the place you choose, give glory to God for his creation. There would be no beach, had He not given the waters a place to come and stop. There would be no churches if there were no God to worship. And no matter the size, make sure, dear one, that you are leaving room for God to attend.

Draw or attach an image of your hoped-for wedding venue below.

*For when God made a promise to Abraham, because He could swear by no one greater, He swore by Himself,*

*Hebrews 6:13*

# THE VOWS

Vow.

A vow, in the case of marriage, is a verb. It is solemnly promising to do a specific thing.

In this case, to bind yourself to your husband and he to you; to love and care for one another; to be faithful to one another; to put each other first.

But, the vows of marriage are not between two entities; rather, they are a promise of three.

When God made a promise in the Bible, there was no higher thing than Himself that he could bind that promise to. When you stand at your wedding, it is to that same power, the God of the universe, your creator, and your heavenly Father that you are holding yourself accountable to.

In a world where words mean less and less on a daily basis, I encourage you to weigh your words today. Whether you choose to write your own, or pick a particular Bible passage to be used during the ceremony, the words you vow, the promises you make, are for a lifetime. Ponder them. Pray over them. Mean them. For you will have to live them.

Do you have an idea of what vows you would choose?

Write down two or three meaningful Bible passages you are considering:

_____

_____

_____

_____

_____

_____

If you wrote your own vows, what promises might you make?

_____

_____

_____

If your husband were writing his vows, what promises would you hope to hear?

_____

_____

How does knowing that your vow is to God as well as your husband impact your thoughts and plans?

_____

_____

_____

_____

Do you consider yourself a person of integrity, someone whose word and promise you only make if you can keep it?

_____

Would others consider you a person of your word? Or would they say you struggle to follow through?

_____

If you have difficulty sticking to your commitments, or keeping promises, take some time to pray today and ask God to help you to take more responsibility in this area.

Pray also for the man God chooses as your husband to be a man of honor, integrity, and trustworthy to keep his word. Evaluate these qualities as you move through your relationship, before you commit your lives to one another.

*Therefore, what God has joined together, let not man separate.*

*Mark 10:9*

# THE BEGINNING

That's right.

The beginning.

It isn't the end.

This wedding you dreamed of, longed for, planned out, rejoiced in, it was not the end goal.

It was simply a day.

A beautiful, special, important, and unforgettable day.

But a day, nonetheless, at the beginning of your journey.

And hopefully, your journey will be less rocky than some because you've taken the time to pray and listen and plan for a marriage, not just a wedding.

# My Dream Wedding

## Plan B

Name: _____

Age: _____

Date: _____

*You are altogether beautiful, my darling; there is no flaw in you.*

*Song of Solomon 4:7*

# THE DRESS.

Describe your dream wedding dress. Is it fluffy? Flowy? Short? Long? Smooth? Sequined? What is the dress of your wildest dreams?

_____

_____

_____

_____

Draw or attach a picture of your dream dress below.

*"Do not let your adornment
be merely outward—arranging the hair,
wearing gold, or putting on fine apparel —
rather let it be the hidden person of the heart,
with the incorruptible beauty of a gentle and
quiet spirit, which is very precious in the sight of
God."*

1 Peter 3:3-4

# THE HAIR.

You have pictured it for ages, admired it on movie stars, been trying out the style in your bedroom. Updo? Curls? Flowing locks? Will it require a full can of hairspray to stay in place? Or are you going for a more relaxed and natural look? What is your wedding hair style?

_____

_____

_____

_____

Draw or attach a picture of your dream wedding hair below.

There is no shame to wanting to look beautiful on your wedding day. But true beauty runs deeper than a pretty dress and flawless hair.

Just as God reminds us not to focus more on our outward appearance than on our inner character, it is also important that we don't fall into the trap of designing a beautiful wedding without any regard to the heart of ourself and our husband-to-be.

Characteristics are defined as qualities that serve to identify a person.

What characteristics do you have that will make you a good wife?

_____

_____

_____

_____

What characteristics do you need God to continue to grow in you?

_____

_____

_____

*"But the fruit of the Spirit is love, joy, peace, longsuffering, gentleness, goodness, faith, Meekness, temperance: against such there is no law."*

Galatians 5:22-23

# The Person

What characteristics, or fruits, will you be looking for in first a boyfriend and eventually a husband? Is he kind? Smart? Sober? Reliable? Gentle? Strong? Creative?
List as many as you can that are important to you!

_____

_____

_____

_____

_____


Which of these characteristics are NOT negotiable, or absolute must-haves?

_____

_____

_____

_____

*Iron sharpeneth iron; so a man sharpeneth the countenance of his friend.*

*Proverbs 27:17*

# The Wedding Party

Bridesmaids, groomsmen, flower girls, and ring bearers oh my!

Make a list of who will stand with you on your big day, and then ask yourself, do they support your relationship with your soon-to-be-partner AND with God? Do they speak truth to you? Encourage you?

_____
_____
_____
_____
_____
_____
_____
_____
_____
_____

*"and having shod your feet with the preparation of the gospel of peace;"*

*Ephesians 6:15*

# THE SHOES

Heels? Flats? Wedges? Barefoot? Foot jewelry? Let's hear it. What kind of shoes do you imagine walking down the aisle in?

_____

_____

Better yet, draw or attach a picture of them below.

Now consider your feet, on which those shoes will go. Which direction are they taking you? Toward God or away? When you get into any relationship, this should always be a question you ask yourself, are you being led toward God, or away? If away, you need to put on some running shoes instead and get out of there ASAP!

*The grass withers, the flower fades,
But the word of our God stands forever."*

*Isaiah 40:8*

# THE FLOWERS

Silk? Fresh? Roses? Lilies? Red? Pink? Yellow? Blue? There are so many options. List your first choice for flowers below.

Bride's Bouquet: _____

Wedding Party: _____

Flower Girl Basket: _____

Boutonnieres: _____

Decorations: _____

Reception Centerpieces: _____

Draw or attach an image of your bridal bouquet below.

No matter which you choose, beautiful though they may be, they will not last forever.

The fresh will wilt; die.

The silk will fade, or be put away in a dusty attic.

Their fates are as numerous as their petals.

But as Isaiah points out, the word of God is forever.

Have you been in the word?

Have you spent time with God concerning your future?

Is it written on your heart?

What about the heart of your spouse?

Pray that God provides a man of God's own word, someone who can encourage you and study with you, learning God's will for your lives as you grow together in faith. Write that prayer below.

*The flowers appear on the earth; The time of singing has come, And the voice of the turtledove Is heard in our land.*

*Song of Solomon 2:12*

*Let us come before His presence with thanksgiving;
Let us shout joyfully to Him with psalms.*

*Psalm 95:2*

# THE MUSIC

Oh, the music! An opportunity to set the tone. Traditional? Uniqu?. Special songs with special meanings? DJ? Playlist? Pianist?

Your choices may be hard to make, listening to song after song and trying to pick a favorite, or you may know without a second thought what you want played during every part of the ceremony.

Music for guests to be seated? _____

_____

Music for family to be seated? _____

_____

Music for flower girl and ring bearer? _____

_____

Music for wedding party? _____

_____

Music during bride's entrance? _____

_____


Music as bride and groom exit? _____

_____


Music to be played at reception? _____

_____

_____

You may have your own ideas about the best music, but don't forget to check in with your groom when you are finalizing wedding plans.

His ideas may surprise you.

*In His hand* are *the deep places of the earth;*
*The heights of the hills* are *His also.*
*The sea* is *His, for He made it;*
*And His hands formed the dry land.*

*Psalm 95:4-5*

# THE VENUE

Have you pictured the place where you will stand before family and friends and receive a new name? Is it the church you grew up in? A beautiful beach holding special memories? Indoors? Outdoors? Large and spacious? Small and cozy?

Indoors/Outdoors? _____

Location: _____

Large/Small: _____

No matter the place you choose, give glory to God for his creation. There would be no beach, had He not given the waters a place to come and stop. There would be no churches if there were no God to worship. And no matter the size, make sure, dear one, that you are leaving room for God to attend.

Draw or attach an image of your hoped-for wedding venue below.

*For when God made a promise to Abraham, because He could swear by no one greater, He swore by Himself,*

*Hebrews 6:13*

# THE VOWS

Vow.

A vow, in the case of marriage, is a verb. It is solemnly promising to do a specific thing.

In this case, to bind yourself to your husband and he to you; to love and care for one another; to be faithful to one another; to put each other first.

But, the vows of marriage are not between two entities; rather, they are a promise of three.

When God made a promise in the Bible, there was no higher thing than Himself that he could bind that promise to. When you stand at your wedding, it is to that same power, the God of the universe, your creator, and your heavenly Father that you are holding yourself accountable to.

In a world where words mean less and less on a daily basis, I encourage you to weigh your words today. Whether you choose to write your own, or pick a particular Bible passage to be used during the ceremony, the words you vow, the promises you make, are for a lifetime. Ponder them. Pray over them. Mean them. For you will have to live them.

Do you have an idea of what vows you would choose?

Write down two or three meaningful Bible passages you are considering:

_____

_____

_____

_____

_____

If you wrote your own vows, what promises might you make?

_____

_____

_____

_____

If your husband were writing his vows, what promises would you hope to hear?

_____

_____

_____

How does knowing that your vow is to God as well as your husband impact your thoughts and plans?

_____

_____

_____

_____

Do you consider yourself a person of integrity, someone whose word and promise you only make if you can keep it?

_____

Would others consider you a person of your word? Or would they say you struggle to follow through?

_____

If you have difficulty sticking to your commitments, or keeping promises, take some time to pray today and ask God to help you to take more responsibility in this area.

Pray also for the man God chooses as your husband to be a man of honor, integrity, and trustworthy to keep his word. Evaluate these qualities as you move through your relationship, before you commit your lives to one another.

*Therefore, what God has joined together, let not man separate.*

*Mark 10:9*

# My Dream Wedding

## Plan C

Name: _____

Age: _____

Date: _____

*You are altogether beautiful, my darling; there is no flaw in you.*

*Song of Solomon 4:7*

# THE DRESS.

Describe your dream wedding dress. Is it fluffy? Flowy? Short? Long? Smooth? Sequined? What is the dress of your wildest dreams?

_____

_____

_____

_____

Draw or attach a picture of your dream dress below.

*"Do not let your adornment
be merely outward—arranging the hair,
wearing gold, or putting on fine apparel—
rather let it be the hidden person of the heart,
with the incorruptible beauty of a gentle and
quiet spirit, which is very precious in the sight of
God."*

1 Peter 3:3-4

# THE HAIR.

You have pictured it for ages, admired it on movie stars, been trying out the style in your bedroom. Updo? Curls? Flowing locks? Will it require a full can of hairspray to stay in place? Or are you going for a more relaxed and natural look? What is your wedding hair style?

_____

_____

_____

_____

Draw or attach a picture of your dream wedding hair below.

There is no shame to wanting to look beautiful on your wedding day. But true beauty runs deeper than a pretty dress and flawless hair.

Just as God reminds us not to focus more on our outward appearance than on our inner character, it is also important that we don't fall into the trap of designing a beautiful wedding without any regard to the heart of ourself and our husband-to-be.

Characteristics are defined as qualities that serve to identify a person.

What characteristics do you have that will make you a good wife?

_____

_____

_____

_____

What characteristics do you need God to continue to grow in you?

_____

_____

_____

*"But the fruit of the Spirit is love, joy, peace, longsuffering, gentleness, goodness, faith, Meekness, temperance: against such there is no law."*

Galatians 5:22-23

# The Person

What characteristics, or fruits, will you be looking for in first a boyfriend and eventually a husband? Is he kind? Smart? Sober? Reliable? Gentle? Strong? Creative?
List as many as you can that are important to you!

_____

_____

_____

_____

_____


Which of these characteristics are NOT negotiable, or absolute must-haves?

_____

_____

_____

_____

*Iron sharpeneth iron; so a man sharpeneth the countenance of his friend.*

*Proverbs 27:17*

# The Wedding Party

Bridesmaids, groomsmen, flower girls, and ring bearers oh my!

Make a list of who will stand with you on your big day, and then ask yourself, do they support your relationship with your soon-to-be-partner AND with God? Do they speak truth to you? Encourage you?

_____

_____

_____

_____

_____

_____

_____

_____

_____

_____

*"and having shod your feet with the preparation of the gospel of peace;"*

*Ephesians 6:15*

# THE SHOES

Heels? Flats? Wedges? Barefoot? Foot jewelry? Let's hear it. What kind of shoes do you imagine walking down the aisle in?

_____

_____

Better yet, draw or attach a picture of them below.

Now consider your feet, on which those shoes will go. Which direction are they taking you? Toward God or away? When you get into any relationship, this should always be a question you ask yourself, are you being led toward God, or away? If away, you need to put on some running shoes instead and get out of there ASAP!

*The grass withers, the flower fades,
But the word of our God stands forever."*

Isaiah 40:8

# THE FLOWERS

Silk? Fresh? Roses? Lilies? Red? Pink? Yellow? Blue? There are so many options. List your first choice for flowers below.

Bride's Bouquet: _____

Wedding Party: _____

Flower Girl Basket: _____

Boutonnieres: _____

Decorations: _____

Reception Centerpieces: _____

Draw or attach an image of your bridal bouquet below.

No matter which you choose, beautiful though they may be, they will not last forever.

The fresh will wilt; die.

The silk will fade, or be put away in a dusty attic.

Their fates are as numerous as their petals.

But as Isaiah points out, the word of God is forever.

Have you been in the word?

Have you spent time with God concerning your future?

Is it written on your heart?

What about the heart of your spouse?

Pray that God provides a man of God's own word, someone who can encourage you and study with you, learning God's will for your lives as you grow together in faith. Write that prayer below.

*The flowers appear on the earth; The time of singing has come, And the voice of the turtledove Is heard in our land.*

*Song of Solomon 2:12*

*Let us come before His presence with thanksgiving;
Let us shout joyfully to Him with psalms.*

*Psalm 95:2*

# THE MUSIC

Oh, the music! An opportunity to set the tone. Traditional? Uniqu?. Special songs with special meanings? DJ? Playlist? Pianist?

Your choices may be hard to make, listening to song after song and trying to pick a favorite, or you may know without a second thought what you want played during every part of the ceremony.

Music for guests to be seated? _____

_____

Music for family to be seated? _____

_____

Music for flower girl and ring bearer? _____

_____

Music for wedding party? _____

_____

Music during bride's entrance? _____

_____


Music as bride and groom exit? _____

_____


Music to be played at reception? _____

_____

_____

_____

You may have your own ideas about the best music, but don't forget to check in with your groom when you are finalizing wedding plans.

His ideas may surprise you.

*In His hand* are *the deep places of the earth;*
*The heights of the hills* are *His also.*
*The sea* is *His, for He made it;*
*And His hands formed the dry land.*

Psalm 95:4-5

# THE VENUE

Have you pictured the place where you will stand before family and friends and receive a new name? Is it the church you grew up in? A beautiful beach holding special memories? Indoors? Outdoors? Large and spacious? Small and cozy?

Indoors/Outdoors? _____

Location: _____

Large/Small: _____

No matter the place you choose, give glory to God for his creation. There would be no beach, had He not given the waters a place to come and stop. There would be no churches if there were no God to worship. And no matter the size, make sure, dear one, that you are leaving room for God to attend.

Draw or attach an image of your hoped-for wedding venue below.

*For when God made a promise to Abraham, because He could swear by no one greater, He swore by Himself,*

*Hebrews 6:13*

# THE VOWS

Vow.

A vow, in the case of marriage, is a verb. It is solemnly promising to do a specific thing.

In this case, to bind yourself to your husband and he to you; to love and care for one another; to be faithful to one another; to put each other first.

But, the vows of marriage are not between two entities; rather, they are a promise of three.

When God made a promise in the Bible, there was no higher thing than Himself that he could bind that promise to. When you stand at your wedding, it is to that same power, the God of the universe, your creator, and your heavenly Father that you are holding yourself accountable to.

In a world where words mean less and less on a daily basis, I encourage you to weigh your words today. Whether you choose to write your own, or pick a particular Bible passage to be used during the ceremony, the words you vow, the promises you make, are for a lifetime. Ponder them. Pray over them. Mean them. For you will have to live them.

Do you have an idea of what vows you would choose?

Write down two or three meaningful Bible passages you are considering:

_____

_____

_____

_____

_____

_____

If you wrote your own vows, what promises might you make?

_____

_____

_____

If your husband were writing his vows, what promises would you hope to hear?

_____

_____

_____

How does knowing that your vow is to God as well as your husband impact your thoughts and plans?

_____

_____

_____

_____

Do you consider yourself a person of integrity, someone whose word and promise you only make if you can keep it?

_____

Would others consider you a person of your word? Or would they say you struggle to follow through?

_____

If you have difficulty sticking to your commitments, or keeping promises, take some time to pray today and ask God to help you to take more responsibility in this area.

Pray also for the man God chooses as your husband to be a man of honor, integrity, and trustworthy to keep his word. Evaluate these qualities as you move through your relationship, before you commit your lives to one another.

*Therefore, what God has joined together, let not man separate.*

*Mark 10:9*

# THE BEGINNING

That's right.

The beginning.

It isn't the end.

This wedding you dreamed of, longed for, planned out, rejoiced in, it was not the end goal.

It was simply a day.

A beautiful, special, important, and unforgettable day.

But a day, nonetheless, at the beginning of your journey.

And hopefully, your journey will be less rocky than some because you've taken the time to pray and listen and plan for a marriage, not just a wedding.

www.ingramcontent.com/pod-product-compliance
Lightning Source LLC
Chambersburg PA
CBHW070943080526
44589CB00013B/1622